MAR 1 0 2005 DATE DUE		
MAY 17 2005		
JUN 15 2005		

Guess Who
Changes

Sharon Gordon

***B*ENCHMARK *B*OOKS**

MARSHALL CAVENDISH
NEW YORK

Here I am!

My mother left me
on this leaf.

I am inside this tiny egg.

I am ready to hatch.

The egg pops open.

I crawl out.

It is easy with 16 legs.

I have become a caterpillar.

I am so hungry!

I eat and eat and eat.

Now I do not fit in my old skin.

It splits open.

A new skin is inside.

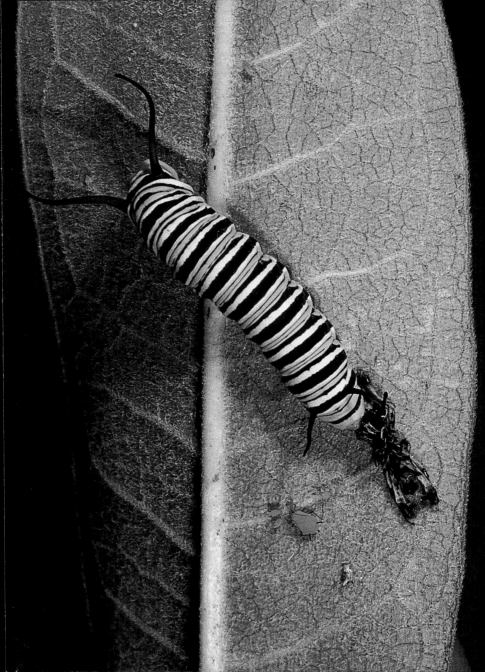

I keep eating and growing.

My old skin falls off each time.

One day, I crawl under a leaf.

I shed my skin for the last time.

A hard shell grows around me.

Now I am a *pupa*.

Inside, I am changing.

I am growing four wings.

My hard shell splits open.

See how I have changed!

I stretch my colorful wings.

I am ready to fly.

Who am I?

I am a butterfly!

Who am I?

caterpillar

egg

pupa

skin

wings

Challenge Word

pupa (pyoo-puh)
A caterpillar that has grown a hard shell on the outside.

Index

Page numbers in **boldface** are illustrations.

About the Author

Sharon Gordon has written many books for young children. She has also worked as an editor. Sharon and her husband Bruce have three children, Douglas, Katie, and Laura, and one spoiled pooch, Samantha. They live in Midland Park, New Jersey.

With thanks to Nanci Vargus, Ed.D. and Beth Walker Gambro, reading consultants

Benchmark Books
Marshall Cavendish
99 White Plains Road
Tarrytown, New York 10591-9001
www.marshallcavendish.com

Library of Congress Cataloging-in-Publication Data

Gordon, Sharon.
Guess who changes / by Sharon Gordon.
p. cm. — (Bookworms: Guess who)
Includes index.
Summary: Clues about the butterfly's life cycle, physical characteristics, and habitat lead the reader to guess what animal is being described.
ISBN 0-7614-1558-0
1. Butterflies—Juvenile literature. [1. Butterflies.] I. Title.
II. Series: Gordon, Sharon. Bookworms: Guess who.

QL544.2.G67 2003
595.78'9—dc21
2003001664

Photo Research by Anne Burns Images

Cover Photo by: *Visuals Unlimited*/Rick & Nora Bowers

The photographs in this book are used with permission and through the courtesy of: *Visuals Unlimited*:
pp. 1, 25, 29 (right) Rick and Nora Bowers; pp. 7, 17, 29 (left) Dick Poe; pp. 9, 28 (upper left) Wally Eberhart;
p. 11 Bill Beatty; p. 15 John Gerlock; pp. 19, 27, 28 (bottom) Bob Wilson; p. 21 Gary Meszaros; p. 23 D. Cavagnaro.
Corbis: p. 3 Jim Sugar Photography; pp. 5, 28 (upper right) George Lepp. *Animals, Animals*: p. 13 Patti Murray.

Series design by Becky Terhune

Printed in China
1 3 5 6 4 2